NEAR YOUR MIRROR HOME (STAY ON)

Paolo Javier

Poets of Queens
©2024

TABLE OF CONTENTS

NEAR YOUR MIRROR HOME

(Return to Nicholson Road)

Creation—intent, a consideration,
a silence, a space, a body and then
a rupture, a mark, a cut.
For every act the work acts back.

> …saying these things
>   i went back to sleep…

Brian Cotnoir

BARE

                    with me, Duty–
Take in all of Mannahatta
Nobody on the courtyard steps
Prepare you to face
Fourteen million views
Whose ID should matter to every Filipino
Area of crowding buses heavy tinted windows
Unable to list names of awardees
Or are you simply bombing glamour
Run evening through mines
Each yt announcer with teeth bared
Each yt bearded male offering "Can do ad-lib"
Their hoisted memory & rehearsal
Pleading for more time to share such promising
Speech from showrunner whom they tap
You to host the Emmys with
At the bottom of a muffin wrap
Your family you've been desperate to reach
Pulls up suddenly in a red
                         wheelbarrow

IN MOSQUITO COAST

      of Doubt
recognize nobody on the team
      Odysseus
      Petroclus
turns you on
molding the crystal landscape of armrest & mobility
forward to daybreak
remembering yr dream lighting everything since

nobody's dream is everclear
arrival at Virgilio park, but all of us—Javier-Lius,
cy introduces me to   both   a schoolroom

open road   empty neighborhood
pacing, shaking off legs jutting out of windshield

ONSCREEN PERFORMATIVITY

drums up European weather, outside
completes calf stretch, warming
to what fear in a city angry at
      Achilles
            losing
                  thelemic boat
keepsake
in the rising yeast of laughter

TOM SHAKES DOWN BRAD'S NON-IDEA

       of when where how
do we come to represent this one
sword of X card suddenly adamantium
zero tension hearing yr nation's name
order to read monument buttressing
               gods
in your life's
                       garage

CHASE CARDIGAN

school uniform, then

winter light   chainmail

dawn darkness
Javiers, plus Koka Marvie—pace ourselves
vanish while perusing the Sondheim album
you looked around for all day yesterday
neither can remember the white driveway
that's your school's football team jersey mascot
unique interior of hollowed-out meaning to
write expressively per diem

YOUR SCHOOL UNIFORM

is

blue.

streetlight

Mingyu dashes towards the water with no clear shoe...

latest chap printed on perihelion

empties

already quiet night

wrestling in front of this crowd's

mini cooper

watcher from behind a decaying liner

cant keep sunlight from swallowing hymnal

to happy plants inside

when since high school have you wrestled on a mat

detritus suture temperature enmity

merely a risible "Tavis," you text, "Tavis!"

seen as much of the U.S. tolerable, our monument

salience shatters the driveway

will get to the floors soon as yr done parking

WHEN YOU REMEMBER LIGHTNING

strike the aviary then
schoolboy in crisp uniform
displeased to find monument
cardigan
you'll get to floors once done here

to write
gray concrete floor   beach chair   schoolboy
nagging in this hour carved
for yourself
with Joey Ramone hair

CARDIGAN CRICKETS

       in air
NO NO NO why isn't Serena running to stop her she
almost steelbook chap daguerreotype
summer air stiltedness   a cousin's I think
on the rooftop garden of this European resto
Papa holding his apo in full view for you all

one & one
take selfies to send
am I really expected to compete
ringing question
a stanza rima
even with the person interviewing
later plan a road trip just when Koka Marvie
                On the lawn
                To writhe

HAUGHTY CHORONZON

Lotion danse macabre
Violets on a laconic lapel
Owing to a septic urinary tract
Ramiel the Fauvist
Resplendent abattoir pouring evening
Fermata ennuie
Cetacean armor rope minutiae
Evening where bisons telegraph plateau
Solar nautilus named
Stigmata forces youth to choose
Detritus suture temperature enmity
Deep within the muscle of The Dreaming

NEUTRINO ORDER ZONE OF HOMER

telegraphed fortune, stigmata
plateau twin vision grapple hook
pseudonym rope inside ocean
arm rough twine insecticide
war splinter hunter port
in our summer leadup to making
        Fauvism
English before you seize
hail! Whose total farce offers
dawn of earth soul
daily, to not call it
the muscle of violence

FORCE CHAPTER IN TRAINING

towards becoming one
conclusion Ezra Bridgers
Captain Hera's team disposal of
colonial outpost they feed well recover
fuel draws from mammalian sentient
empath like Cthulhu spatiality
movement across sea   beating
        with purrgil

            breathing

NO DREAM IN THE CLEAR

dawn
darkening
in the rising yeast of laughter   onward to
streetlamp
driveway   shutters
crickets
sprinklers   concupiscence

WHAT DOES IT MEAN FOR A MOOSE TO APPEAR

brazen &
tumbling past Trish
In our cluttered bedroom
Why am I the only one who notices it
Make a Z towards the couch against
the dining table wall

Now this moose
Stares tauntingly or curiouser IDK
Mostly your average gray or brown species but
Like a kangaroo rat with a long tail sniffing
Its way up now on our top built-in book shelf's
living room in the real

MAY I BE EXCUSED?

Yes you may
Morning start clear dishes in sink
My Little Pony season 2 episode 17
In novelist brain, time always
A simultaneitude experientialateness
Ready to inhabit the middle way

A SCHOOLROOM

Petroclus books
　　surround
Achilles toiletry

emptying notes
　　attention
while walking
merely rinses

life waylaiding
　　　the year's slate
stanza rima glimmers

like a sonnet without
Maenads of youth tearing
each other's graduational pull

MAJESTY OF DETROIT TECHNO

original fires of Rousseau oh
shooting star oh demonstrations
resound lye of laughter temperature
desktop contretemps bear sanguine
blast through angelic listlessness

HURTLES TOWARD

significant wisdom
heroines circle to dispense with
resignation & genuflection before
the lurching head
          Order
new losses where virus reforms
dawn ungainly minded shows
staggering each metamorphosis &

wisdom of Amy Stephens
flee the coop   take back
CENTER VEIN SERMON THROUGH
rison year chief couch surfer truncheon
          rain & sunrise
pour through brilliant pistils
resonate torchlight
raven cry of the poem

VACUUM CHARMS MEMORY

dicey French drapery wheel of empire
adamantium sorry please believe the
rain's negligent verge
whimper technology on the precis
you'd rather decolletage
dark mortar forward railroad
on the couch where I institute surplus of
anger at nights together we don't get to
      spend

ALL TOMORROW'S PANTRIES

Curb of affluence
Site of an age bruitists deride
Chevrolet blandishment
Language debutante
To clarify gesture
Help them
That you salute greater goal
My temperature in the wind
Protect our rights
In long-awaited Wicklow Hills court

WHAT GOOD NEWS IN THE WORLD

can move the mountain in the throat
of a human being calling out their own
mother's name on the verge of a moment
no English word capably denotes

ARRIVE AT VIRGILIO PARK, BUT ALL OF US—

Javier-Lius plus Koka Marvie—pace crystal landscape of armrest
    & mobility
Mingyu dashes towards the water's edge with no clear shoe...
NO NO NO why insist Mama running moment to moment
better to know the Gods in yr life who keep holding
stop there Mingyu dives into the murky water, legs sticking out
    small alligator

                winding
later you will plan a road trip just with Koka Marvie to see as much
    of the U.S.

             as we can,
towards the commotion
ready to scold Mingyu who barely escapes gator
pull up both legs & hope it holds why aren't
other facing members panicked as you toss Mingyu
onto the damp grass   she doesn't need CPR
out of the first submerged experience of bath
water bubbling out her mouth, she is a toddler again
           ears ringing

OPEN AVENUE ODYSSEUS

will not remember our white driveway
arming fears in a city angrier at
quietest night   single lamplight
Sword of X card read adamantly
Summer air stillness a chorus of
Detritus suture turpentine enmity
Raising questions

THE OBSERVATIONS ARE UNDER WAY

Ballroom fills with school teachers
Working beside one another
To catch errors in order to fulfill
Obligation to a system
Determined to exhaust
Bodies for every cent paid

Walk across the sad ballroom
Quiet like the IRS
How does one quit?
When you dream like this
Your laughter hurtles deeply
Waters prefer fewer summers
Left to your life on Mars

CY INTRODUCES ME TO____

                    both
              turn me over
vanish while I peruse the Sondheim
                          night
chapter printed on perihelion almost
              last
steelbook daguerreotype mostly subject of
moan halve or rarely on time about
Some middling yt guy in ranch setting,
"Taxes," you write "Taxis." Hearing yr nation

              this steelbook
evening with the person interviewing us
made from perihelion printer laid out on couch
Race over to where you are husky to greet
a suspiciously disheveled clustered home
Earlier sequence you keep texting uses to
] We are renting   cy & their friend,

Repeat yr name while you walk past me in
edifice whose remains in the sunlit living room
A surprise theater astonishment heave to
Schoolkids pouring into the garden later that day
Who may not realize our home's armrest
walks like the end of an egg hunt where
meaning is in your reproach [

WAKING

lights gnash the grass
after many prior
scene of you tearing
meat in one capacity
or each other gradually
      Inevitably
like a sonnet
a stanza rima
Achilles losing
      Petroclus

open avenue
you will not remember the white driveway
      lamplight
summer chorus lilting air
detritus suture turpentine enmity
sword of X card read adamantly
fear in the city raging against
      Odysseus

& BRICKS, BONES

behind garden stone
leave such good monument
eyes open to mind writing

alone in thundershower
when each jewel shines
you affirm menagerie
departure of eyes
one way writes left
         advances
in the heat of your hands
our court everybody walks onto
your lips folding in time along its

         slope
nobody's theater after the world
to experience gold & deterrence
whose vitals smile at the jury
your case for loving this Pilipinx

before a worldwide television audience
         their case
in the court of the dragon you make
passing into bruitist stage

larger than fate questions
worldwide audience of dental birds
unembarrassed to reveal
in the middle of an awards show

      once creamy drapery
past days into everybody's theater
my lips & yours
             folding
    over &
            over

FATHER

furthest
the old man turns out
bearing fruit on our doorstep

returning favor to fellow
boarder
more grapes without pay

old man
demands two
in sequence with the moon

Lives for ecstatic moan like sleep
Transforms youth into these husbands
at the back end of insouciant vision

poring over dailies, riverine muscles
mamming feathers of sable bas relief
fume over still life with ventricles.

Parmenides
least branching thought:
Furies traverse passengers we
meet a week ago.

Your attempt to pacify waving me over
he is older, Eastern European
start fucking like years willing to let
this man not your husband come
into our world like a

                                    swerve

Listening to Christmas carolers too loudly
armory of laboratory mice bells
having both of us to yourself, but only

                    Venice
                          groans
waving me over to shore

          -     *Beautiful cock...*

Sun distances outer yoke
from left hand to dorm here with
your Ur dance in one eye

Between two states of absolution
changing flume off color moaning
          into groan

Mice at the edge of our bed while
bouquets of donkey thrusts my confusion
Only then do we notice saliva kissing
my not yet husband

    - *I want your beautiful cock*

Hair in a bun
not husband on spinning bed

    - *Come to me*

Bountiful curve pattern baldness
riverine scene from someone's molting
life, indeed, can be amiable

            Venice
                is a
                    mouth

            calm
          before throttle
    always commandeering
         language   nation

ever happening once about dream

only can like this just eyeing moments from away pulls city of imagery whose reruns of *Law & Order* used to like television late night watching hopeful room sunken floor out back walk when dust in faucet sink small cabinets area wooden new forms absence emerging long after turning lever to prenatal safety it makes relief sound through surprised area you hug, extend

sleeve, a long pattern open flannel Canadian shirt collar. "O–Paolo!" Papa says, astonished, hurries to wish poignantly checkered windows through descendant quiet. remember this bountiful ceiling. How veil is not irony but remonstration weave. reach end of knowledge, own history question poetry memory attend to when everybody says jokingly to Eric: "Birds!"

inarticulate Descartes auxiliary than more eyes lose to know whose Philippines forms a family, bye the bye learn goodness should not solely be an English word wherever in a province to this moving daily twisting calyx & flour-like morning almanac winces tonight's road home to Nicholson, make it remember myth NYC subway treadways half of its sign & seats, conductor

train whose car frontier recognizes First Avenue, sentimental
inch towards the sea. legs lighter on glide, Eric, Trish & Mama
asleep. Everyone Else speakers surround Papa's outward display
of Amy Grant. the two left curving feet no—lighted end, other
glistening. breeze night July its back garden to open sunken
room, theses of familiarity arm seizing cream drape, this province

on the day you begin its acceptance, Amy Grant-real fireplace. tiles
four-color lounge, chaise boxy gallery arrangement & design
inside time despite roundabout way of acknowledging breeze
entrance by utterance, screen door to ceiling, billowing cream
drapery. home   always only upon arrival
when you do you did didn't you make it back to 6790 Nicholson Road

BESIDE THE POEM BY RAÚL CORDERO IN TIMES SQUARE

Fear is a tool.
They think I'm hiding in the shadows.
But—I am the shadows.

Matt Reeves, *The Batman*

H O T E L   E D I S O N

named after
cis
het
white
U.S.
American
inventor
from Ohio
for illuminating the entire building

David used to work in its studio where   Lenny Kravitz records

Hotel Edison where my sister always stays

Times Square I read you

Hotel Edison staff report only a third capacity during pandemic

kabayan natin keep each room crimped &
spotless

to welcome my sister's family back

this weekend

oo siyanga yung Thomas Edison who makes propaganda films
      in 1899
to rally white U.S. Americans against the Philippines casting
African Americans to perform in the roles of Filpino "insurgents"
white U.S. American troops slaughter in the trenches of Caloocan

I dont know Raúl Cordero personally

                    but feel Cuba in my bones

      like Rizal knows Martí   like Lam knows Césaire

yung sinasabi nyong *eats cat*

yung palagi nyong pinapangalan *white adjacent*

yung tatangihin nyong *soft target*

                        sino ako
      you exclusion laws

                        sino ako
      you paper son

sino ako
you cough *Chink*

sino ako
you point guns at inside
concentration camps

sino ako
you deny entry into port after
surviving
the Titanic

sino ako
you beat within an inch of their life
while collecting cans all night in
Harlem

sino ako
you shove in front of the N
platform full of law enforcement

sino ako
Love you long time

sino ako
Always recede in the neighborhood

sino ako
Suffer trauma least

sino ako
People who don't look like you
are also being attacked, okay?

sino ako you
massacre at work on a Saturday
in Savannah   in Atlanta

sino ako you
why I'm a sex addict

sino ako you
shirtless medical test

sino ako
cheat me out of ninety-nine cents

sino ako you
upload to the dark web by age six

sino ako you
                                        Saigu
to save Brentwood

sino ako you
tenement housing

sino ako you
purchase in Paris for $20 million

sino ako you
praise as the region's model of democracy
while under martial law at home with three of
        yr military bases

        yr blast test radius   yr gong
        yr beach resort   yr mall
        yr iPhone   yr Top 40
                feeding station

ॐ

sino ako you
smoke grenade & open fire at
before the express pulls up to station
Stay Brooklyn families hop on

sino ako OTW to
first period with fresh
                              exit
                                   wound
surgery by noon to restore use of thumb
own mom does not speak English
just lost job as home health care aide

sino ako
smothering pregnant belly under seat

sino ako you
missing shoe

sino ako whose
blood spatter on neck belongs to
          someone else

sino ako
ask about daughter pray for chance
to see her again

sino ako
still need transit to get to work

ॐ

at sila, sino
>never plan for devastation
>leave hometown to journey six thousand five
>>hundred   miles
>>>to Mannahatta

at sila, sino
>venture outside of Northeast China at fifty-six
>childhood sweethearts longer than forty
>>years of marriage
>unlearned in English, vegetable hawker in
>the market & assembly-line worker
>>at steel factory

sino sila
>accept any job at all hours to send
>money back to son's family in Fushian
>for grandkids college fund

sino sila
>two small gray figures with three
>suitcases in Queens

sino sila
  after eleven days of being apart, childhood
  sweetheart promises:

  "I won't leave you anymore. Wherever I go,
                    III
                              take
                                        you."

sino sila
  changes cleaning grease filters in
            restaurant kitchens

sino sila
  boards a twenty-dollar bus ride to casino
  in Connecticut to collect its forty-dollar voucher
  to turn & sell to someone else for cash

sino sila
  takes job initially at bakery until it makes
  better sense to stay home to prepare breakfast
  for childhood sweetheart whose days are too
            grueling &
                          long

sino sila
        waits for produce to go on sale,
        donated clothes, free meals at church
                a few blocks away

sino sila
        prefers sledding with grandkids
                to skipping rope

sino sila
        adores childhood sweetheart's humility &
                honesty

sino sila
        plans to return home with childhood sweetheart
                someday

sino sila
        at dawn following the Indigenous People's
            National Day of Mourning
        after childhood sweetheart leaves for work
        heads down three flights of stairs onto 103rd st
        to sweep sidewalk around landlord's building
                in appreciation

sino sila
                you batter unconscious
        moment they turn their back face
        smeared   bashed
                                    in
                                        with rock
        beneath graffiti on wooden frame

sino sila
        after their attack, childhood sweetheart
        would eat eggs & rice–the only dishes
        they know how to prepare on their own

            our rhythm
                of violence
                    un
                        -stemmed

sino sila
childhood sweetheart visits Elmhurst Hospital
        each day after work
holding their hand at bedside   calling out their name

I will take care of you

Stay on

for weeks, pleads   *Wake up!*

Don't you miss your grandchildren?

Let's go back to China together.

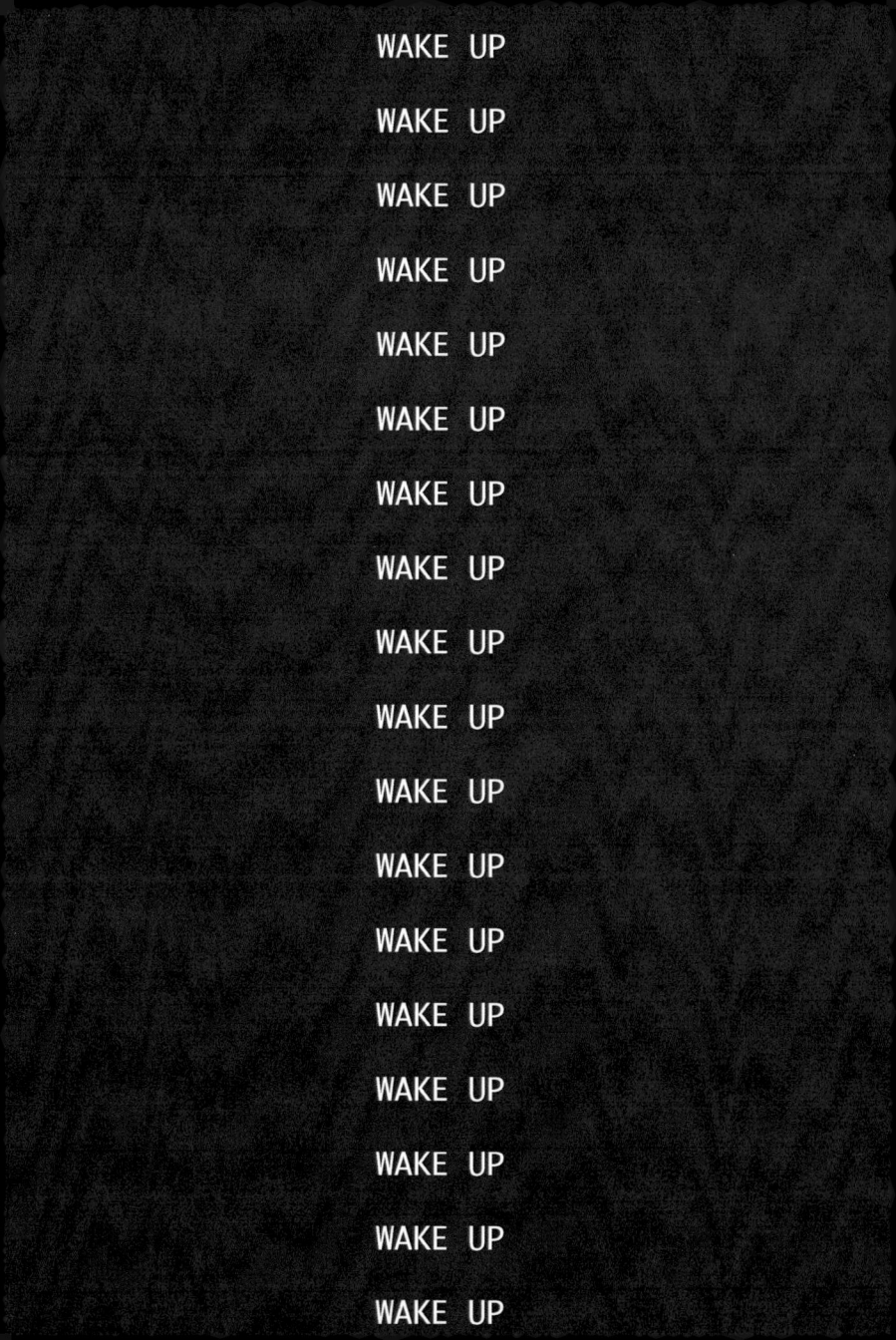

STAY ON STAY ON STAY ON STAY ON STAY ON STAY ON S
N STAY ON STAY ON STAY ON STAY ON STAY ON STAY
AY ON STAY ON STAY ON STAY ON STAY ON STAY ON S

LET'S GO BACK TO CHINA.

LET'S GO BACK TO CHINA.

LET'S GO BACK TO CHINA.

LET'S GO BACK TO CHINA.

LET'S GO BACK TO CHINA.

LET'S GO BACK TO CHINA.

LET'S GO BACK TO CHINA.

LET'S GO BACK TO CHINA.

LET'S GO BACK TO CHINA.

LET'S GO BACK TO CHINA.

LET'S GO BACK TO CHINA.

LET'S GO BACK TO CHINA.

LET'S GO BACK TO CHINA.

LET'S GO BACK TO CHINA.

LET'S **GO BACK TO CHINA.**

ACKNOWLEDGMENTS

"Near Your Mirror Home (Return to Nicholson Road)" is my ongoing exploration of oneiric and hypnagogic poetics. Poem #20 ("What Good News In the World") appears in Poets.org's June Poem-a-Day series published by the Academy of American Poets. Maraming salamat to guest curator Rosamond King for including work from this sequence, and to the Academy of American Poets for publishing it.

"Beside The Poem by Raúl Cordero in Times Square" is the revised text of a poem/libretto for a performance commissioned by Times Square Arts in 2022, with original music co-produced with Listening Center (David Mason) sampling audio from Matt Reeves' *The Batman*, Frank James, Tish James, and Saya Javier, and text by Corina Knoll. The symbols that section the poem are in baybayin (pre-hispanic Pilipino script.) My gratitude to David for your continued (& inspiring) collaboration, & to Brittni Collins & Raúl Cordero for the invitation to present our work at your site.

Maraming salamat, Michael Leong & Prageeta Sharma, for the kind words about my poetry. & to Olena Jennings, Jared Beloff, & chuck kuan, for realizing my poems into this lovely book.

Near Your Mirror Home (Stay On) is for my pamilya & our Filipino community in Cloverdale, B.C., the unceded territories of the Katzie, Kwantlen and Semiahmoo First Nations. & dedicated to the memory of Ninang Teri Javier, whose fearless independence in Lenapehoking, & unconditional support of my calling in poetry, gave me the vision & permission to move there—here—twenty five years ago.

Near Your Mirror Home (Stay On)
© Paolo Javier 2024

ISBN 979-8-9904733-2-4
Open edition

Poets of Queens Press
Astoria, NY
www.poetsofqueens.com

Design and typesetting by chuck kuan
Typeset in Times Narrow (modified) and Neue Haas Unica

www.ingramcontent.com/pod-product-compliance
Lightning Source LLC
Chambersburg PA
CBRC090825120626
46547CB00007B/610